ALSO BY ANN HAMMOND

POETRY

October
Selected Poems
Hear the Kingfisher
Places Called Home
Sea Wings

ANTHOLOGIES

Old Furrows
She Returns
Swans and Armchair

ON HIGGINS BEACH

New Poems by
ANN HAMMOND
With a Foreword by Molly Peacock

To Josh,

In celebration of Amelia's
80th birthday June 30th, 2019
With every good wish.

Ann r Emily.

Designed and produced by:
Maine Authors Publishing
12 High Street, Thomaston, Maine
www.maineauthorspublishing.com

Printed in the United States of America

In gratitude to

Molly Peacock
Friends at Higgins Beach
Friends at Piper Shores

CONTENTS

FOREWORD
By Molly Peacock

I heard a wide ribbon of a voice calling out to me, hearty and British, and turned to see that it came from an athletic woman a good head taller than the other poetry-lovers who were milling about after my lecture at the Unterberg Poetry Center of the 92nd Street Y in New York City. It was 1998, almost exactly twenty years ago. "As a teacher myself," Ann Hammond said, "I appreciate good teaching."

Poetry, like music, is sometimes taught in an apprenticeship system. An established poet takes on private students to learn techniques, arcane ones sometimes, and Ann came to me after that lecture with a proposal to learn the sonnet. When a teacher—in her case a worldly one who had taught in Africa as well as the United States—becomes a student as an adult, there's a high bar set for the person who instructs her. I pulled up my socks. Rapt, determined, armed with a rich, open energetic laugh at her beginner's mistakes, Ann set about becoming an apprentice sonnet-maker.

Athletes have an appreciation for discipline and its joys, and Ann, who had taught physical education and was herself a great walker and swimming enthusiast, had an instinctive enthusiasm for the forms of poetry. Sonnets have a special feel that can be similar to a saltwater swimming pool—a miniature ocean. Ann plunged in, making sonnet after sonnet, and then upping her game to crowns of sonnets (a linked series, the first line the same as the last). She made me recall that the Dutch philosopher Johann Huizinga linked poetry with sport. In his book *Homo Ludens* he proposed that play—with its rules that replicate and miniaturize the greater world within a set of boundaries—was the basis of poetry.

But what had play to do with the serious subjects of Hammond's earlier poems? It was childhood. Often her subjects in those years of apprenticeship writing were events from her girlhood in England during World War II. The post-traumatic stress disorder she still suffers from echoes back to the bombs of the blitz. Poetry, because it is an act of memorialization, provides a way to process the past by using it as raw material. Verse repatterns the past simply by the fact that lines and stanzas pattern language. Like someone learning, then excelling, at breast strokes, back strokes, butterfly strokes—not to mention high dives—Ann set about gaining expertise, all the while mining memories.

And then, as happens when a poet gains a certain level of excellence in a strict form such as the sonnet, Ann broke loose. Suddenly couplets, triplets, free verse, indirect rhymes—the whole bag of poetic tricks—opened up for her. She began matching all kinds of forms with all kinds of subjects, including relationships, contemporary life, and animals, too. Poetry became a way of studying human nature and nature itself.

Vigorous, strong and strong-minded, she wrote on, stopping to collect her poems into books—now her sixth. These volumes track one woman's pursuit of understanding through a vivid rhythmic note-taking that involves observing that world, confronting failures, and laughing with a hard-earned flexibility. We don't think of flexibility as being earned, but after a certain age, one must train for it, and paradoxically, relax for it. *On Higgins Beach*, her latest collection, provides a template in poetic form for just this apparent contradiction. The opening poem, "Angel of Mystery," presents us with a snowy owl, blown off course to Maine, that stares "with gold eyes" "from an old cedar roof." The poet wonders whether it is (as Hammond learned from her life in Africa) a Kikuyu "harbinger of death," or simply an animal seeking to right its course, a "messenger" for how to do just that. The poem joins both ideas, and sees a strength in those "white wings" that the speaker now is "ready to fly on," whatever the destination, including a final one.

On Higgins Beach, with its poems about advancing age, turns from the remembrances of her previous books toward the texture of life as it is lived daily, now. A walk on the beach, the bark of a dog, a drink at a fireside, an intimate conversation, all exist in a sea of moment-to-moment awareness inside current living. Anyone who has read the work of Ann Hammond or encountered her personally knows that there are two necessities in the Hammond life (and in the Hammond book): a dog and an ocean. The endlessness of the ocean, with its own rhythms and overwhelming presence, is Hammond's element in *On Higgins Beach*. Her poems sail the ocean, and she steers them into and out of storms. Ebullient canine

friendship infuses her poems with a sense of obser-
vation from another worldview—an animal view—
with humor, lightness, and a dogly (or is that godly?)
joie de vivre.

Another animal, a monarch butterfly, closes the
book in a deft sonnet titled "Black Spindly Legs."
Like the insects in the haiku of Issa, the Japanese poet
who so empathized with animals that they seemed
to communicate with him, the butterfly climbs on
Hammond's hand as she rescues it, "a patch of wet/
sand stuck fast to one wing." The Monarch manag-
es to stay "still on my hand" as the poet actually gets
into a car and proceeds to drive "carefully/to a garden." There the butterfly climbs off onto a "two-
lobed/fragrant snapdragon."

Hammond knows well that metaphor, by vir-
tue of its comparison nature, produces its own wis-
dom. She ends her book with this wish for the "fragile survivor":

> I hope she drinks nectar to celebrate
> her endurance and to ease the night ahead.

In Hammond's poems the valuing of natu-
ral experience, even as extraordinary an episode as
this one, does not fend off death, but makes the
transition into the next world a deeply rich and con-
scious one.

Often the first moment of a relationship—its
birth—makes a template for interactions to come.
"As a teacher myself, I appreciate good teaching,"
became a signpost for me. Ann signaled that she
had something to teach me, even as she asked me
to instruct her in the intricacies of poem-making. I

have long thought that creating a poem can never be perfect; a poem is like a ceramic pot or a wood-crafted cabinet, a hand-made object. Therefore, it comes with certain flaws—flaws that in some ways make it all the more valuable. As I watched Ann transform into an artist—for that was what all our one-to-one lessons at first in person in New York City and now long-distance on the telephone between Toronto, where I live, and Ann's adopted Maine are about—I realized that a simple request to learn a verse technique was in fact much more.

However, if she had said, "Teach me to use my imagination to craft things in lines, images, and sound that have never existed before, teach me to take my voice so that it renders into words a tone and a time and a lyric moment that won't be replicated and will outlive me," I certainly would have refused. After all, that was what I was teaching myself! (And stumbling about learning, too.) Yet that's exactly what happened—for both of us. In many ways, both Ann and I are self-taught. Let me put it this way: self-taught in the presence of others. I certainly can say to her, through watching her learn and understanding how her example has instructed me, "I appreciate good teaching." In *On Higgins Beach,* a poet's life choices structure her poems. Inside the supporting grid that wraps sentences around lines and collects those lines into stanzas, Ann Hammond takes on the matter of how to live gracefully into a buoyant advanced age.

November 1, 2018
Toronto

ACKNOWLEDGMENTS

My thanks to Molly Peacock, who has mentored me for twenty most wonderful years. Her fine teaching, encouragement, and sensitive guidance have given me the joy of writing poetry in my retirement years.

For discovering me as a poet, having belief in my work, and publishing *October* and *Selected Poems* in the Bookman Press, my gratitude to the late Barbara Wersba.

Many thanks to Canio's Books in Sag Harbor for hosting all five first readings and sales of my poetry books.

Thank you to Elizabeth Saltonstall, watercolor artist, for providing the beautiful painting on the cover; and to Maine Authors Publishing for designing and publishing *On Higgins Beach*.

Frontispiece photograph courtesy of Piper Shores.

ANGEL OF MYSTERY

Are you a spirit guide? I know
your silent puffed image haunts me daily.

I'm talking to you snowy owl, with feathers
fluffed, perched still as an egret waiting.

Now far from your Arctic home, you've chosen
to watch the beach from an old cedar roof.

Did the last Nor'easter bring you to Maine?
Some Kenya Kikuyu believe you must be

a harbinger of death. It's true a friend's
obituary came the day you flew here.

This famous author who gave me
the love of poetry (hidden for decades)

calling it "my golden vein." Now snowy owl
with gold eyes looking straight in to my blue,

is this your call for my spirit to fly
home? Glorious, if you're the messenger—

for you are beautiful. So when you're ready,
I'm ready to fly on your strong white wings.

THE SHARD

The shard of green glass I found in the sand
this morning, carved by rock, wave and time,
was once a beer bottle. This jogs my mind

to the day I sang "ten green bottles," in a Luton
air raid shelter—then emerged to find
the hat factory bombed, leaving straw and ribbons

on the trees. Now here is this pummeled glass
fragment, ready for an artist to fashion
into a mobile, or necklace. A green

bottle battered to beauty by craftsmanship.
The final vision like peace, after horror
of war. So, what of the person who drank

this bottle? Was it thirst, a celebration,
or compulsion? Yesterday, I had my
first beer in sixty years, at my first ball game.

Beer fitted the occasion, so I may
go to more ball games, to drink some more beer,
thus perhaps cause an artist's treasure.

THE SURFERS

When downgraded hurricane waves whip Maine,
they give Higgins Beach some challenging surf.
I watch black silhouettes flat on boards time
their dives through breaker arches; and they look
like tadpoles, who change into jumping frogs
when they catch the right wave. They remind me
of our friend my mother called "rubber pants,"
a brave Undersea Fighter, who planted black
limpet mines (ever so quietly) on sides
of enemy ships during WWII.
These young men this morning, who catch sunlight,
waves and joy, are far from those silent nights
of secret raids. And I sit here grateful
for frogmen who helped create waves of peace.

IN THE HUSH

The trail through the wood to the beach today
is edged with buttercups and Lady Ferns.
The path opens in to a small ancient
apple orchard, where the trees are twisted
with gnarled joints like carefully carved sculptures.
This spring afternoon a strong onshore breeze
has whipped up the surf.

                              Still, my favorite
times are sunrise and sunset. I dream
God opens her eyes over the horizon
and at dusk closes them. At night nature
takes a long deep breath. A time when prayer
or meditation in the hush becomes
an opportunity to listen, may-
be find some truths which we may need to know.

LAST CARTWHEEL ON THE SAND

This morning I was loaned a collection
of last poems. It had me thinking. Would

I know when I wrote my last poem? Would
I sit down and say, "now I will write my

exit poem." I doubt it, as I live
as if my days will never end. Each new day

brings me one of the delightful small things—
the way my dog studies me at first light

to know what we will do next? She takes her clues
from the clothes I put on, my old brown jeans

mean we are off to the beach to greet friends,
hers and mine. It's true, I cannot remember

when I flung my last cartwheel on the sand
or jogged for two miles. It's enough to know

I'm able to walk three miles, hear the cardinal
hidden in a tree, and watch for cloud signs

of changing weather. So, this had me thinking,
when did any howl deep inside me vanish?

EBB TIDE

Layers of gentle waves roll in,
reminding me of a frilly
petticoat, or tutu skirt
of pink and pastel blue,

color of tonight's muted sunset.
Then comes the orange moon rising
above the horizon to challenge
our perception and wrongly believe

the horizon moon to be larger
than the zenith moon. The way
I thought you to be quite different
in nature than now you have shown

yourself to be. So, like some past
astronomers, it's time to refocus
my perception, and to convince
myself to see a new view.

EMILY'S EXAMPLE

What I can say is I'm a nature lover,
without doubt a poetry lover and deep
lover of the sea. It's somewhat in doubt
whether I may call myself a people
lover. Though the friends I love, I love deeply.
I find some people disappointing. Do
you? Anyway, I resolve to donate
my pedestal to Good Will. Then meditate
on my faults, to be kind for at least a week.
This will mean taking long walks by the ocean
with the greatest lover of all, my dog.
A Havanese who adores everyone—
who does not growl at folk. Do adopt her
example, Ann, for Emily knows best!

VIEW OF THE ATLANTIC

Do words dry up? Does imagination?
At my community I join a group
for dinner. They choose not to converse,
I begin to chat, there is no response—

My words dry up like a wrinkled prune.
Does there come a time when we have nothing
more to say? As a poet, I fervently wish
to be spared from losing word power.

I gaze out the window to watch the surf fly
as it meets jagged rocks at high tide.
At eighty, each day
                        becomes a new kind
of challenge. In the quiet I welcome waves
of inner guidance, as I swim for the shore.

GADABOUT

To fry in a heat wave at two airports
last June, with long lines weaving like pythons
on pot means I'm happy to hang up my
travel shoes. So, I'll make Maine my last port.
As I walk alone at the beach today
the sea mist rolls in and wraps around me
like a safe squishy shawl in harmony
with the wash of the waves and gulls' cries.
Yesterday, two friends and I hiked the cliff walk
and enjoyed the same views as Winslow
Homer painted. I pointed out his studio
as we passed by, and thought how well anchored
I was among rugged rocks. Yet—sea spray
may awake my gadabout quondam gene.

GREAT WHITE PYRENEES
ON THE BEACH

He was dreaming of the great times he spent
at the seventeenth century court,
till he was woken from his reverie
for his early morning beach walk.

Now he lumbers toward a large lump of kelp
nosing aside some slippery slimy
fronds, until he finds his favorite, the stipe—
a dog whole-wheat spaghetti appetizer.

Half heartedly in a British accent
his owner shouts, *"Monty, no!"* No response.
He's been trained "to keep calm and carry on,"
so keeps on chewing, pawing, and chewing.

At last Monty does come, and we resume
our walk until sunrise. The time when we
say "ttfn," and Doug gives his one arm
hug, and I know it's a day well begun.

SHIVER ME TIMBERS

After a storm at Higgins Beach
sand often shifts to reveal rib
tip remnants of the three-masted
schooner, *Howard G. Middleton.*

This 1897
largest wooden sailing ship
smashed off the coast of Maine—
how Ya she must have looked

under full sail. Now this salt soaked
deadwood wreck reminds me of a pre-
historic Sea Monster. I search next
to this skeleton for a lump of coal

from the cargo that never made it
to Portland. Middleton in dense fog
under full sail, went off course, sadly
struck a rock near the eastern side

of the Spurwink River bluffs. The strike
bored a huge hole in the hull,
then the enormous boom fell.
The spar clipped Captain Shaw's wife who

fell overboard and was washed out
to sea. This hundred year loss marked
by the ship-grave in the sand—And
where the ship's bell rings on foggy nights.

FEATHERS AND PAWS

1

"Golden plover on toast," was offered
on the first *Titanic* breakfast menu.

Until hunting was banned in New Orleans,
forty thousand plovers were killed in one day.

The small piping plovers have a nesting
area on the sands of Higgins Beach.

Faithful volunteers try to protect them.
At night, they remain in danger from foxes

raccoons, even feral cats. Large gulls like
to feast on the eggs and chicks. At full moon

high tide may wash away their nests. However,
this year seven fledged and soon will fly south.

2

My elder brother drew pictures of birds,
gave me a book he made when I was five.

So, on my desk stands a photo of the snowy
owl, next to one of my service dog.

They both can be seen at Higgins Beach. One
often, the other a rare sight; I treasure both.

THE RETURN

You wear a wide brown police belt buckled fast
on the first notch—your waist thin as the few
hours you rest a day. I feel your ribs poke
through your shirt as we embrace. Those fourteen
hours a day working two jobs? Your own goal
to pay off a student loan. It's been two
years since I've seen you.
                              We became fast friends
the day you drove me home, after a beach
bum walked off with my towel, shoes and car keys.
I was so hot in the sun, a small boy
offered me his soda. Then you were there,
knight in black regulation police serge. Now
you are back, giving out parking tickets. So,
look for me. I vow to bring you good snacks.

SUNRISE AND FRIENDSHIP

You are way down the beach.
As you walk toward me with

Teddy, your dear black-and-white
dog, I recognize you

by your short red jacket.
I'm happy you are here,

and look forward to your
genuine hug, which warms

any freezing windy
day here at Higgins Beach.

The sunrise matches this fond
spirit of our beach bonding,

while ease of our friendship
mirrors a calm sea.

TOWELS AND CHAIRS

Early morning, friends or family members
arrive at the shore to select coveted

sand estate, by placing towels and chairs
at the high tide mark. These stay empty

(a sort of beach trust) until their group gathers.
This leaves the early morning dog walkers

to weave round the objets d'art, to avoid
adding to their colorful decoration!

I use my supernatural voice control.
Mostly, Emily will "come," that is,

unless she finds a smelly pile of seaweed,
or meets her best friend Penny dachshund.

IN WINTER

There is a blizzard howling,
a Nor'easter blowing fifty

miles an hour, and snow expected
to reach eighteen inches today.

We had a wonderful white Christmas,
and an ice storm that made all the trees

sparkle. How I love Maine in winter:
hot toddies, log fires, and brisk beach walks.

QUITE ENOUGH TO SATISFY ME

"I want to be your rock," you said.
Do you know you passed it on
to me, and I stand on it now?

True my white hairs increase, and so
do goodbyes to family and oh,
so many friends. In the practice

of letting go, I have gifted
furniture, books, and past keepsakes.
For I accept there are "no pockets

in my shroud." Loss becomes
familiar, while fear becomes an
empty shell burning white in the sun.

Though I do wonder about new waves
of loss. The kind where I might not see,
hear or remember? Leaving earth

in a sudden sea storm would be
more to my liking. My thoughts roll
in rhythm with the outgoing tide—

where I see a pink glow mirrored
in the flying surf of the sunrise,
and welcome a new unframed day.

RETURN OF THE MOCKINGBIRD

On an early morning walk to the beach
with our four dogs, we hear the mockingbird
in full throated song. He is boldly perched
on his chosen lookout, the metal edge
of a "No Parking Anytime" sign! With
the sun on our backs and a mild breeze
ruffling the marsh grass, it does feel like spring.
However, the snow has not melted, it hangs
on in frozen heaps left by the snow ploughs.
There's no knowing how long it will stay,
along with my winter feelings of friends' deaths:
Barry wrote for "Mr. Rogers," Nancy
edited *People* magazine, Barbara
wrote books. Each shared the pen with me.

IN MEMORY
OF BARBARA, BARRY,
NANCY & HARRIET

A well known mystery writer who lived in
Sag Harbor village came to my house one
day to read a romance to my sick
Yorkshire terrier. Her second surprise
was to remember me in her will. This
in turn paid for many poetry lessons.
As the circle continues, friends support
my readings, buy books they don't need, and give
me publishing parties. I see their
footprints in the sand as they walk beside me.
At low tide, I stroll close to the waves and think—
How do I thank famous writer mentors
for sharing their gifts with me? My way will
be to write until a shroud gloves my hand.

BLACK SPINDLY LEGS

Danaus plexippus, Monarch Butterfly

I found this fragile survivor near
the waves, wings open with a patch of wet
sand stuck fast to one wing, anchoring her
until the tide would end life. When I put
my warm finger near the black spindly
legs, she climbed on tight to this chance
for life and clung. This monarch beauty stays
still on my hand as I drive carefully
to a garden, where I find the two-lobed
fragrant snapdragon flower (*Antirrhinum*)
and gently lift my treasure to a pink
petal. Her wings open and close twice.
I hope she drinks nectar to celebrate
her endurance and to ease the night ahead.

ANN HAMMOND was born in England in 1936. When she was three years old World War II began, which had a profound effect on her childhood. Ann, her mother, and brother moved from town to town trying to escape German bombs while her father served as captain of a Cable & Wireless ship.

Educated in boarding school and London University, she moved to Rhodesia before immigrating to America in 1964. For forty years she taught health and physical education in private and public schools while earning an MA from Adelphia University and becoming an American citizen in 1972.

At the age of fifty-eight she joined her first writing group, a workshop given by author Barbara Wersba, who encouraged her to write poetry. She has studied for many years and currently studies with poet Molly Peacock. Ann Hammond resides in Scarborough, Maine, with Emily, a Havanese terrier. She is listed in *Who's Who in the World* 2014.